Buying your affordable dream property in Spain

(A step-by-step guide)

Includes free online Affordability Calculator

Howard Green

Disclaimer: Any information or advice available in this book, videos and spreadsheet is intended for educational and general guidance only. The author shall not be liable for any direct, incidental, consequential, or indirect damages arising out of access to or use of any of the content made available. Readers are encouraged to seek professional advice tailored to their individual circumstances before making any real estate or financial decisions.

DEDICATION

This is dedicated to all the dreamers
who dared to look for a slice of paradise
and act.

"Whatever you think you can do or believe you can do,
begin it.
Action has magic, grace and power in it."

— Johann Wolfgang von Goethe (clearly not a Spaniard, but still)

ABOUT THE AUTHOR

Howard Green grew up in Yorkshire, England. He currently lives in London and dreams of retiring to Spain.

Buying Your Affordable Dream Property in Spain is a guide based on the experiences of the author and his wife. Trained in finance in the property industry, the book combines the author's love of Spain with financial and property expertise. It is written to guide prospective buyers through the unexpected, helping to make informed and financially sound decisions.

When not writing, Howard enjoys running, listening to music and photographing his travels.

CONTENTS

FOREWORD

Decision-making is the most important skill you've never been taught.

So, how do you avoid making bad decisions? Preparation of course! By buying this book you've recognised this need and you're in the right place to learn what's different about buying property in Spain. The objective is to share insights into the real process, potential challenges, and tips to make informed decisions. You'll better understand the local market, legal requirements, potential investment opportunities, and most importantly of all, your budget for your piece of paradise.

I'm excited to share my personal experience and professional insights with you from buying a property in Spain along with my wife. This is a real dream come true as we've been visiting Spain together for over 20 years and somewhat suffer from procrastination! We have visited all four corners of Spain and have rented many properties, particularly in the south, so we have a wide appreciation for the Spanish lifestyle and are happy to finally own a property in Málaga, Andalucía (Costa del Sol).

As an accountant and finance manager for over 15 years, I've had the opportunity to work in the residential property industry, providing financial analysis and advice. We have also successfully bought and sold several homes and investment properties in the U.K. over the years. This unique blend of personal and professional experience is what I've drawn on in this process and am now sharing in this book, so that you may better know what to expect during the process of buying a property in Spain, and importantly, to **know what you can afford from the outset. The included online 'Affordability Calculator' will help you quickly calculate your approximate budget** and will automatically apply the correct taxation rate for your chosen area, as well as the live Euro exchange rate to convert your funds from any currency.

I hope it's an enjoyable and exciting journey for you.

A note on terminology, the following terms are used interchangeably:

- Real estate and property
- Estate agent and realtor or real estate agent
- Lawyer and solicitor
- Conveyancing and buying a property
- Apartment and flat

Let's embark on this exciting journey together.

1 - THE BUYING PROCESS, STEP-BY-STEP

Welcome to your journey of buying your affordable dream property in Spain!

This book is your friendly guide through the entire process. Starting with your property search through to receiving the keys and living in your new home.

We'll walk through each step, share practical tips, and simplify your budget calculation with the included "Affordability Calculator". So, let's get started on turning your Spanish dream into reality.

Chapter overview

2. **Initial property search**: Begin by researching areas, property types and prices online to see what budget you may need.

3. **Calculate your Realistic Budget**: The central objective of this book, from which all other steps follow. What you need to know

about how banks calculate mortgage affordability, what it will cost you and how much deposit you will need. The online Affordability Calculator is included with your purchase and guides you through the calculations.

4. **Mortgage – agreement in principle**: Confirmation of how much you can borrow.

5. **Estate Agents - informed property search:** Engage with local estate agents to find suitable options, armed with your Realistic Budget.

6. **Lawyers:** How to figure out the most suitable one for you.

7. **Reserve your property & NIE application**: Signing the reservation agreement takes the property off the market while your lawyer conducts due diligence and applies for your NIE number. There is different advice out there about when to apply for this as it can take weeks if you do it the slow way….

8. **Private Purchase Contract & final mortgage application:** The PPC (Contrato de Arras) is a pre-agreement of the eventual purchase. The bank valuation of the property should be booked after the reservation agreement (step 7) is made, so the required funds are confirmed prior to signing the PPC.

9. **Completion - Notary public:** On the completion date, you (or

your representatives with Power of Attorney) meet the seller and their representatives, plus your bank's representative at the notary's office to sign the title deed (Escritura) of sale. Also, the remaining balance is paid. Then the notary transfers ownership to you. Time to celebrate, but leave some cash for the taxman......

10. **Renting out the property**: Managing agent fees, Spanish income tax, tourist licence, budgeting.

Each step may vary based on the region the property is in and your individual circumstances. Consulting with legal professionals and real estate agents is crucial to reducing the risk of expensive problems and aiding a successful property purchase in Spain.

THE BUYING PROCESS, STEP-BY-STEP – BONUS VIDEO

(Scan QR code on your phone)

2 - INITIAL PROPERTY SEARCH

The first step to owning a piece of the Spanish dream is diving into the initial property search. It's an adventure begun by a single click on a website. Then, you hit the streets of your chosen area, casually browsing estate agent windows. Before long, your question, "¿why not?" is answered with "¡Vamos!" to act and make it happen!

•   **Online Research**: Explore property websites and portals to get familiar with availability in your chosen area. Test your criteria, such as location, size, features, and the budget range required. This will give you the confidence to proceed.

•   **Estate Agents:** Spain is less dominated by national companies than England. Focus on larger estate agent offices with properties suitable for foreign buyers. These offices will generally have more

English-speaking staff, too. They often offer useful insights about the local market and inform you of recent sale prices. After meeting a few, you'll get a sense of which agents will be most helpful to you. See below for more details.

- **Property Portals:** Use property portals such as idealista.com/en, ThinkSpain.com, Fotocasa.es/en, and Kyero.com to explore a wide range of properties in Spain. These portals often allow you to filter properties by location, price, size, and other criteria, such as balcony, terrace, or swimming pool!

- **Property Exhibitions and Events**: Useful for new ideas in the early stages. You can meet developers, agents, and other industry professionals. You can also find out about upcoming new developments and ask questions about the local property market.

- **Local Newspapers and Magazines**: These often have a section dedicated to property listings and feature upcoming new developments.

- **Word of Mouth**: Talk to family, friends, and work colleagues who have owned property in Spain. Their experiences and knowledge can help you gauge realistic valuations.

Spanish estate agents' websites have done a lot of catching-up in recent years, and the quality of information has dramatically improved. It's common to find floorplans, 3D floorplans, and even video tours of properties, saving you time on wasted visits. The more properties you assess, the more confident you will be about valuations in your search area.

When looking at property listings, you may see the price per square meter for the built area or usable area. Usually, agents quote the larger (built area), including walls and unusable space, sometimes including balconies and storage rooms. When comparing figures from different agents, it's important to make allowances for these differences in calculation methods. To calculate the price per square meter yourself, divide the property's asking price by the area quoted. To ensure a fair comparison, use like-for-like figures to avoid comparing apples with oranges – although they do taste delicious here!

Comparing price per square meter can be used as a broad indication of value when comparing similar properties in the same area. In cities, these values will scale exponentially near the most prestigious districts. So, values quoted on portals, such as idealista.com/en/data/ should only be taken as rough guides.

idealista/data   Investors Banks and Servicers Developers Appraisers Agencies Others 🌐 English ▾

Everything you need to know about the real estate market

We put our data-driven analysis services within reach of any real estate professional.

| Request more information | Watch video |

Latest reports on the real estate market

| 📄 Monthly residential market report - Spain April 2024 | 📄 Monthly mortgage market report - Spain April 2024 | 🏛 Quarterly mortgage market report - Spain Q1 2024 |
| We analyze the main indicators of demand, from mortgage firms, non resident mortgages and subrogations, | We analyze the main indicators of demand and mortgage firms, as well as their evolution over recent months. An | We analyze the main indicators of demand, from mortgage firms, non resident mortgages and subrogations, |

View all reports and studies on the real estate market

3 - CALCULATE YOUR REALISTIC BUDGET

The initial property search is like a rollercoaster of emotions - exciting possibilities, beautiful properties with dream-like features, but then the fear of missing out, reality checks, and concerns that this isn't affordable set-in (or was that just me?!).

One of the most significant differences between buying property in Spain versus the U.K. is much higher taxes. The property transfer tax in Spain will be around 7%-12% of the purchase price (depending on the region and whether it is resale or new-build)! In the U.K. it's currently 0% up to £250k, and then from £250,001 to £925,000 it's still only 5%.

And that's not the end of the pain, as there will be notary, land registry, and other admin fees totalling another few thousand euros. Solicitor fees are commonly 1% of the purchase price in southern Spain. In fact, 1% seems to be a favoured pricing method for various professional services rather than a fixed-fee related to the amount of work involved. In the case of mortgage brokers, for example, shop around. More on that later.

All in all, you need to budget around 2-5% on top of the property transfer tax that applies in your region, so 9%-15% overall. Of course, you can't get a mortgage for these costs so your savings will need to cover this and your deposit. Quite considerable additional costs compared to the U.K.

You're going to need a chunky deposit.

As a non-resident, the currently available highest loan-to-value (LTV) of Spanish mortgages is 70%. So, overall, you're going to need about **39%-45% of the property price in cash / investments**. This can be funded from your savings and investments but needs to be accessible in time for the completion date.

This is where the online 'Affordability Calculator' comes in to save the day, which is included with your purchase. The Calculator allows you to quickly estimate the savings you'll need for the deposit and also perform the initial affordability check that Spanish banks will use on your application. The Affordability Calculator has been designed with non-financial people in mind, so don't be put-off by the spreadsheet.

Follow the 'How to' video linked below and take it step-by-step.

Let's make some quick calculations to get on firmer ground and put some foundations underneath this dream!

Login to your Google account and type the URL into your browser to open the **Affordability Calculator**:

https://tinyurl.com/SpanishAffordabilityCalculator

Scan the QR code to follow the step-by-step tutorial video on how to use the Affordability Calculator:

AFFORDABILITY CALCULATOR - VIDEO GUIDE

(Scan QR code on your phone)

4 - MORTGAGE APPLICATION IN PRINCIPLE

Once you have seen some properties and are comfortable you will find a suitable one, begin the mortgage application process. Engage a mortgage broker or apply directly to the banks for a mortgage up to the maximum amount you expect to need, based on the Realistic Budget you calculated.

The objective here is to confirm that at least one bank will offer you the required mortgage amount. Then, you can engage with estate agents and explain to them that you're serious buyers with the funds in place. This is an advantage in a strong property market where properties are selling in days. It also avoids having to pay a deposit on a property before being sure you will get the mortgage.

After agreeing to buy a property, the actual mortgage offer will depend on the bank's valuation survey of the property you are about to purchase. But let's not get ahead of ourselves!

The mortgage approval threshold has risen since the Great Financial Crisis of 2007-8. The days of saying, "Yeah, I can afford this", are over, and nowadays you must prove you have sufficient income for the foreseeable future.

Completing the affordability checks and using the online 'Affordability Calculator' (covered in Chapter 3) ensures your finances broadly align with banks' criteria.

Mortgage Brokers

Whilst you might not need to use a mortgage broker in the U.K., it can be advantageous as an overseas buyer in Spain to use one. While some banks are English-friendly (e.g. CaixaBank has an English portal amicably named 'HolaBank'), most application forms are in Spanish.

A good broker's expertise goes beyond language skills. They have in-depth knowledge of which banks will be most suited to your circumstances and how best to present your application. This is especially useful for those with complex or unusual financial circumstances.

If you're a bargain hunter like me, you'll want to get comparison offers to select the best deal. Unlike the U.K., banks in Spain may negotiate on rates and opening costs. A broker can leverage multiple offers to negotiate better rates, which could save you thousands over the term of the mortgage.

Lastly, by delegating the form-filling, we saved time for the more exciting task of viewing properties!

Instructing a mortgage broker

Since 2019, when Spain applied the EU credit directive and made it law, all mortgage brokers (Intermediarios de Creditos Inmobiliarios) have to become qualified by sitting the Spanish mortgage broker exams and register with the Bank of Spain, which is the regulatory body for all financial institutions in Spain. The Bank of Spain has a register that lists all regulated financial institutions.

You should check on the Bank of Spain web portal that your mortgage broker is registered (only enter the first name of the person you are dealing with):

https://app.bde.es/rbe_spa/#/buscador

Unless your broker is called Francisco, there shouldn't be many results.

You can also ask your broker for a copy of their public indemnity insurance. This covers themselves (and therefore yourselves) should you need to take legal action in the unlikely event of a mistake costing you financially. More importantly, it means that the insurance company is likely to have also conducted some due diligence on the broker. Checking reviews of the broker online is useful but can't be relied on to be 100% genuine.

You may prefer to use an English broker based in Spain for clarity of communication and an appreciation of the differences between English and Spanish mortgages.

We contacted three brokers before settling on one from the fairly large number available online. You'll get a feel for who you want to work with by performing the due diligence described above and discussing the mortgage process with the broker. They will ask questions about your income, savings and required mortgage (not requiring any documentation from you initially). In return, they should be able to indicate your likelihood of getting the mortgage amount requested - and whether it is worth proceeding with the application.

Only provide all the required documentation to the broker once you have done your due diligence. After all, by definition, this is all the documentation necessary to take out a mortgage in your name – so you want to make sure it is only supplied to legitimate entities. Identity theft can happen, so take precautions. Also, once the process is over, you may want to request that they delete all the confidential information they hold about you. In their Terms and Conditions, there should be a section in their data policy about the deletion of client data.

Whether you are applying directly to the banks or via a mortgage broker, you are likely to be asked for the following documents (original PDFs, not scans of printouts from the internet):

- Passports.

- Bank statements (6 months minimum, depending on the bank).

- Statements of your deposit holdings (e.g. savings & investments).

- Statutory Credit Report, e.g. Equifax or Check My File, free of charge. Apply for this before leaving the U.K. as you may need to receive a security letter in the post.

- Utility bill for proof of address.

- For employees: Employment contract, P60 for past two years, payslips (6 months), possibly tax returns if you have non-employment income.

- For business owners: Proof of income for the past 2 months (invoices), past 3 years tax returns.

Banks usually charge a mortgage opening fee (aka Arrangement Fee in the U.K.) of between 0.5% and 2%. All the mortgage offers we received had opening fees of 1.5%. However, if you have multiple offers, you may be able to negotiate this down. Agreeing to take (overpriced) life insurance with the bank may reduce this fee and the mortgage rate. You probably will need some life insurance with a Spanish institution in any case, so you'll need to assess which deal is best overall.

The maximum loan-to-value offered by Spanish banks is currently 70% to non-residents. Applicants can be up to 75 years of age at the end of the mortgage term (some banks use 70 years of age). Otherwise, the mortgage term can be 25 years or possibly longer.

The longer the mortgage term, the lower the monthly mortgage repayments and hence the **more likely your application will be assessed as affordable**. If affordability is tight, look at increasing the term as this reduces the percentage of monthly debt repayment to your net income. This needs to be **under 35% (some banks may use only 30%),** including the repayment on your home mortgage and any other properties you own. If affordability is tight, a mortgage broker's knowledge can be valuable in knowing which mortgages to apply for to succeed with your application.

MORTGAGES IN SPAIN - BONUS VIDEO

(Scan QR code on your phone)

5 - ESTATE AGENTS

We discovered several differences between estate agents in Spain and those in the U.K. that are worth knowing about upfront.

Aspect	UK Estate Agents	Spanish Estate Agents
Property Listings	Centralised (e.g., Rightmove)	Multiple portals, less centralised, agent focused
Agent's Role	Primarily seller-focused	Can be more buyer-focused, shared listings
Offer Process	Highest offer usually wins	First acceptable offer may win
Commission	Typically lower (1-2%), paid by seller	Higher (3-5%), can be split between buyer and seller

For context, in 2024, the property market in Málaga was particularly strong, with fairly-priced properties selling within days, often before the property was marketed. This chapter is based on our experience with resale properties in this fast-paced market, the dynamics might differ elsewhere in the country. Prices of new-builds tend to be less flexible, and time-pressure might be reduced for large developments being sold off-plan with plenty of choice.

This chapter explores three key aspects of the search and negotiation process in the Spanish property market, based on our personal experiences. Whilst these insights are primarily drawn from our time in Málaga and may differ in other regions, they offer valuable guidance to help you secure your dream property, steer clear of unprofessional agents, and focus your property search:

Speed Matters: First Acceptable Offer Wins

Firstly, do your research. The worst thing you can do with property is rush. You should have clear criteria for what you want and a sense of market prices. Check out similar properties online before your first viewings, ideally also visiting locations to gain familiarity.

However, being too slow can lead to disappointment. We missed out on a great property because we delayed our offer. We thought it was best to view another interesting property first as we had only just started our property search. We then learned that an offer had been submitted and accepted, and that the reservation contract was in lawyers' hands. This was two days after the property came onto the market!

We found out later that the accepted offer was slightly under the asking price. Because we intended to offer the full asking price we were confused and couldn't quite believe what had happened.

In the U.K., estate agents are only too happy to explain that it's their job to get the best price for their client – the owner – which also maximises their commission. In Spain, at least in Málaga, this is not necessarily the case. If an offer is put forward, then even if there are other interested parties, it may be accepted and the property taken off the market, even to people who have already viewed it.

Another difference is that estate agents will share the level of other offers with you, so don't be shy to ask. Clearly, this is very helpful for the buyer. As this is so different to the U.K., initially we were sceptical, however, our experience so far has shown this to be reliable (see note at the end of the chapter about registered estate agents).

In hindsight, we had been too caught-up in the significance of the reservation deposit and thought that we had to be 100% certain before even submitting an offer. Another agent advised later that we should have made an offer, had the other viewing to be sure and then proceeded with the reservation agreement. We really ramped-up the pressure on our mortgage broker to get an offer from a bank at this point.

Do plenty of comparisons with similar properties to assess the market value of properties you are interested in. Ask agents about prices achieved from recent listings versus asking price. Unfortunately, in Spain there is no public access to the registry of actual purchase prices as there is in the U.K., so you're more in the dark. One way to test this is by offering under the asking price and gauging reaction, but this could mean you miss out on your property. This may only work if you're the first to offer on the property and can afford to increase your offer if needed.

There is no more crucial point than placing an offer. Offering under the asking price by several percent takes some confidence and the estate agent might think you haven't done your homework, so explain what research you've done and say it with conviction. If they price high, it's because they believe they know more than you.

You can still get into a bidding contest, if you are the first to make an offer and it is not accepted by the seller, then other parties may appear with higher offers – as they've been informed by the agent of your offer.

Beyond Rightmove: Navigating Spanish Property Listings

Secondly, in the U.K., Rightmove has been the go-to place for property searches for many years (there is now more competition, but still). All agents feed their details onto Rightmove within hours of marketing a new property. For buyers this is an ideal situation where all you need to do is subscribe to an alert with your criteria and you've got the whole market covered.

In Spain, timely property listings are more fragmented. Rightmove does now have a limited search facility for Spanish properties, but in our experience it is a mistake to expect the same success as in the U.K..

As mentioned earlier in the initial search section, there are several other property portals in Spain (e.g. Idealista, ThinkSpain, Fotocasa, and Kyero), and in our opinion these are currently better than Rightmove in Spain, but they don't appear to be updated as frequently, so check individual agents' websites too. It's still useful to set-up alerts on portals though, especially for notifications of price-reductions.

Before our first property-viewing trip to Spain, we found a promising listing on Rightmove and arranged a viewing. The 'agent' then scheduled visits to four additional properties. However, during these viewings, it became clear that our contact wasn't a legitimate agent but rather someone hoping to share commissions with actual property agents. This can be risky, especially when it comes to paying reservation deposits, as you might not know the other agent involved either. Unregistered agents may use high-pressure sales tactics or provide incorrect information. Check you're dealing with registered, professional agents (more on this in the last section).

It's really common for agents to share their properties and commission with other agents. There's only one registered agent we know of in Málaga that won't share commissions. They also required us to sign a statement confirming each viewing - likely to secure their commission if we bought through another agent later.

The other property we tried to arrange a viewing from Rightmove turned out to be a guy based in the U.K. posting Spanish agents' properties along with his mobile phone number! He used high-pressure double-glazing style sales techniques to try and get us to sign an exclusive agreement with him as he said he covered 99% of the properties on the Spanish market! I can only imagine he was calling-up the real agents to arrange viewings with the intention of sharing commission. I don't recommend going down this route.

However, you could use a local registered agent in this way. If you find an agent that understands your requirements and is willing, you could request they undertake your search – despite not having your dream property on their books. Somewhat like having a property consultant only it won't cost you extra – they will be splitting the commission with the listing agent of the property you buy. This could save you time searching and avoid the headache of arranging multiple viewings with different agents.

The Gatekeepers: Importance of Estate Agents in Spain

Thirdly, estate agents play a crucial role and you need to be proactive in your dealings with them. If you want to be informed about the best properties that are about to come onto the market, stay friendly with the agents! Otherwise, you may only realise what you've missed when you see a great photo proudly stating 'sold' in their office window. This is time consuming because you need to be visiting their own websites and offices when you are in Spain, frequently.

Nowadays it's easier to stay proactive and organised thanks to free communication tools such as WhatsApp, which is heavily used in Spain by the agents and is ideal to receive links to property details, videos, and scheduling viewings.

Especially since 2022, consumer protections have been enforced with the aim of professionalising the estate agent sector. For example, in Valencia, estate agents have to be formally qualified and display their registration at their office and on their website. Here and in other major autonomous regions such as Andalucía and Catalonia, agents must be registered with the local estate agent register for the region. This ensures that they have liability insurance and a physical office address to be contactable by clients.

ESTATE AGENTS - BONUS VIDEO

(Scan QR code on your phone)

6 - LAWYERS

Engaging a competent lawyer for your Spanish property purchase is essential to ensure the transaction proceeds smoothly, the property is legitimate, and to protect you from serious problems such as losing your deposit. We felt that the 1% fee was worthwhile, considering it safeguards your entire investment.

To avoid conflicts of interest, it is advisable to find your lawyer independently of recommendations from your estate agent, developer, or mortgage broker. While some estate agents and property developers may recommend or have 'partners' for convenience, these may not always act in your best interest.

Once your offer to buy a property is accepted, you will want to quickly proceed to signing the reservation contract. It's **very important to have your lawyer review the reservation contract before you sign it**. Therefore, you should look for a suitable lawyer alongside your property search to be ready when the excitement starts!

Your lawyer should be fluent in English and experienced in property conveyancing, not another branch of law. So, you could engage a solicitor based in the U.K. who specialises in Spanish property conveyancing, or an English-speaking Spanish lawyer. Also, a U.K. lawyer now based in Spain, who has built-up extensive experience in the Spanish conveyancing process, could be a good fit.

Finding a suitable lawyer

A good starting point is the U.K. Government website, Gov.uk, which offers a 'Find a lawyer abroad' service:

https://find-a-professional-service-abroad.service.csd.fcdo.gov.uk/find/lawyers

Combined with Google searches and Google Maps, we selected our lawyer. Spanish lawyers are generally open to introductory meetings of 30-45 minutes to discuss their services and fees. We met with three different firms (two in person, one via Zoom) and found that they all presented well at the meeting. However, following up on requests for information varied a lot.

As taxes and fees are a significant part of the total cost of buying a property, we requested an outline of these expected costs. One firm provided insufficient information and was excluded. The other two firms offered different estimates for notary fees, land registry, power of attorney, administrative costs, and NIE applications. Neither mentioned the substantial mortgage opening fee (1.5% of the mortgage in our case).

Verify the credentials of your chosen lawyer through the Census of Lawyers at the Abogacía Española:

https://www.abogacia.es/en/servicios-abogacia/censo-de-letrados/

Enter their first name in the 'Nombre' field and click 'Buscar' to search. Optionally, you can add their surnames in the 'Apellidos' field or their university location in the 'Colegio' field (mentioned on their 'About us' website section), if there are too many results. Ensure their details match your expectations, such as their employer's address.

We chose a firm with a local office for convenience and ease of signing paperwork. It is also reassuring to gauge their availability for ongoing support. While online reviews can be insightful, they should be taken cautiously due to potential manipulation.

Power of Attorney

Discussing the Power of Attorney (POA) led to the longest conversations. Granting significant powers to lawyers in a foreign language contract can be daunting. The first firm we met with was very persistent, encouraging us to visit the notary quickly and sign the POA.

Whilst the notary will translate the contract verbally to you and answer your questions, it won't allow for careful checking of what powers you want to grant when you are already sitting in their office under time (and cost) pressure. We requested a copy of the document in advance, and generally, they were reluctant to do this. This may be because we had not committed to their services or paid anything at that point. We did eventually get a copy which we ran through an online translator and also got two Spanish work colleagues to review. This wasn't the actual version we ended-up signing, so we still had to get the notary and our lawyer to translate the final version to us.

The POA allows your lawyer (and their firm) to act on your behalf without your physical presence, which is particularly useful if you are not in Spain during critical stages of the transaction. The firm's code of conduct usually requires lawyers to contact you before acting on your behalf as a signatory of a document (e.g., private purchase contract, mortgage contract, title deeds) to gain your approval. However, they are not legally required to do so. Therefore, you **should only grant POA to lawyers and not to estate agents, brokers, the friendly property developer etc**. Lawyers have professional indemnity insurance, providing recourse for restitution in the unlikely event something goes wrong.

In the U.K., POAs are typically associated with managing affairs if you become mentally incapacitated or pass away. While you will not grant such broad powers to a Spanish firm of lawyers for the conveyancing process, the concept of granting powers is similar.

You can rescind the POA by visiting any notary in Spain, or asking your lawyer to arrange it, or simply returning the original POA document to you (they always need the original to utilise the POA). The POA can include a time-limit clause expiring after the property purchase completion date. This is the most hassle-free route and allows you to forget about it. Handy!

The POA can be limited to the conveyancing of a specific property, but if the purchase process does not proceed to the private purchase contract stage, you will incur the expense and inconvenience of signing a new POA for the next property you want to buy.

Later, if you are going to be renting out your property, you will likely want your lawyer to administer the ongoing transactions such as income tax returns. This could be covered by a new replacement POA with the necessary powers at that stage.

Fees and Services

We found that most lawyers were charging 1% of the purchase price, with some including IVA (Spanish VAT) in this figure and others adding the 21% on top. The cheapest lawyer we found offered 0.9% including IVA. Check their charging timeline – whether it's 100% upon completion, 50%/50% at the start/completion, etc. Also, ask what would be payable if you reserve a property but have to cancel, e.g., due to a problem found during the due diligence process.

Lawyer's services include:

- General advice and answers to questions about the process and property-specific issues.
- Reviewing the reservation agreement and potentially holding your deposit in their client account.
- Applying for your NIE number.
- Setting up a Power of Attorney for the conveyancing process.
- Reviewing and negotiating the Private Purchase Contract.
- Liaising with the bank/mortgage broker.
- Handling your affairs for the property transfer and completion.
- Ensuring all legal requirements are met during this process.
- Providing tax and financial advice if needed, e.g., tax returns for your rental property. This requires them to have a tax accountant on staff.
- Setting up utilities in your names and with your Spanish bank details.

7 - RESERVE YOUR PROPERTY

Once you have found your dream home and had your offer accepted by the seller, you need to proceed with the following steps:

- Reservation contract (after your lawyer has approved it).
- NIE number application.
- Bank valuation survey / Opening of current account.

Reservation Contract

Under the Spanish conveyancing process, signing a reservation agreement and paying a small deposit is customary to reserve the property from being sold to anyone else (for the time being). This step ensures a commitment from both the buyer and seller, reducing the risk of gazumping and other issues common in the English property market! This avoids delays, expenses, and disappointment caused by buyers pulling out or sellers increasing their price after agreeing to the sale.

Send the reservation agreement to your lawyer for approval before signing or paying anything. Once approved, pay a deposit (this is around 1%-5% for resale properties). This deposit reserves the property while your lawyer conducts due diligence. Your lawyer will add conditions to the reservation under which you are entitled to a refund, such as if they find a problem with the deeds or if you cannot obtain a tourist license for short-term rentals (e.g., Airbnb) from the community of owners. It may also depend on your mortgage being agreed upon, although sellers might not agree to this condition in strong markets. Discuss these conditions with your lawyer. The payment is typically made to your lawyer's or estate agent's client account, highlighting the importance of engaging with reputable estate agents.

NIE Application

Next, have your lawyer apply for your NIE number, which is required for each property buyer. The NIE (Número de Identidad de Extranjero) is your tax identity number. It is essential for purchasing property, opening a bank account, obtaining a mortgage, connecting utilities, and more. The notary will require your NIE on completion day.

In some areas of Spain, there are long waiting lists for NIE appointments (at the local police station), sometimes taking weeks.

Therefore, some property websites advise applying for your NIE as soon as possible, even before you start looking for a property.

Law firms with multiple offices around southern Spain can apply for your NIE number in towns with shorter waiting times, often obtaining it within 1-2 weeks. They will need Power of Attorney (covered in the previous chapter) to do this on your behalf unless you can travel to the appointment. You will likely need to authorise Power of Attorney with your lawyers for the conveyancing process anyhow, so they can simply add the NIE application to the powers to cover this. We paid the notary EUR 140 for both of our POAs, and this allowed our lawyer to avoid the nearly two-month wait for NIE appointments in Málaga.

While searching for a suitable lawyer, we met with three firms, all of whom advised waiting until we found a property before applying for the NIE. This is for several reasons, for example, you need to state the reason for your NIE application, such as buying a property, and provide its address. While you could use the address of the first property you make an offer on, the lawyers we spoke to only recommend this if you are certain you will soon find and agree on a property. Applying for an NIE and not using it may cause issues, and having a different address on your NIE application and residency application can create administrative headaches. If you have dual citizenship, consult your lawyer on which passport to use for the NIE application, as it has implications for taxation on rental income and residency applications later on.

Bank Valuation Survey / Opening of Current Account

After signing the reservation, arrange for the bank's valuation survey of the property. The loan-to-value (LTV) percentage offered by the bank is applied to either the valuation of the property or the agreed purchase price, **whichever is lower**. Knowing the valuation upfront ensures you can obtain the required mortgage amount before committing to your purchase.

Once the valuation report is issued (this typically takes a week to ten days) the bank will issue the binding mortgage offer and open a current account for you.

There is an additional risk in the Spanish mortgage approval process compared to the system in the U.K.. In Spain, you must once again submit your financial statements to the bank prior to them making the final binding mortgage offer. **It is essential to maintain a stable financial position** in-between the time you obtained the mortgage in principle offer and applying to finalise the mortgage. The most significant example would be a material decrease in the net salary shown on your payslips (beyond any variance already explained during your application). **Do not apply for any new debt** during this time and do not make any debt enquiries that result in a new hard-search appearing on your credit history.

In preparation for your property purchase, you should start discussing the transfer of funds from the U.K. to Spain with your U.K. bank. Otherwise, due to anti-money laundering legislation, there could be delays when you request a large transfer abroad. The bank may request proof of the source of your wealth. You don't want this to happen when you are already in Spain. I have heard of a case where a purchaser had to fly back to the U.K. to get the funds released.

Consider using a money transfer service / foreign currency specialist to save on bank fees. Compare with quotes from your bank. A currency specialist will manage the process and advise you on how to minimise currency exchange rate fluctuations affecting your funds. **Ensure they are registered with the FCA** (Financial Conduct Authority).

The two main bank transfers you will need to make after paying the reservation deposit are:

- Funds for the 10% deposit. Transfer to your lawyer's client account. Covered in Chapter 8 – Private Purchase Contract.
- Funds to cover all remaining costs associated with the purchase. Transfer to your Spanish bank providing the mortgage. Covered in Chapter 9 - Completion.

Before making any large transfers, double-check the recipient's bank details in person or over the phone. Do not rely solely on an email for bank details as these can be intercepted and altered by fraudsters.

RESERVE YOUR PROPERTY & NIE APPLICATION - BONUS VIDEO

(Scan QR code on your phone)

8 - PRIVATE PURCHASE CONTRACT & MORTGAGE

Following the due diligence, a private purchase contract (*Contrato de Arras*) is drawn up between the buyer and seller. This will normally be agreed within 15-20 days of the reservation agreement, with the assistance of lawyers from both parties. Your lawyer will review the property's legal status, ownership history, and any potential issues such as outstanding debts or liens.

Upon signing the *Contrato de Arras*, the buyer pays a non-refundable deposit. This is usually 10% of the property price for a resale and 30% or more for new-builds (although this might be staged), less the reservation deposit paid previously.

You need to transfer the deposit funds into your lawyer's client account prior to the signing. You should ensure that your lawyer is registered (see Chapter 6) and using a segregated client bank account for these funds, not their business account. They will then make the transfer to the vendor's solicitor upon the signing of the PPC.

The *Contrato de Arras* / PPC outlines the terms and conditions of the sale and sets an immovable date for the completion of the purchase (usually within 60 days). There may be exceptions to the rule, but you don't want to be in the position of trying to change any of the terms retrospectively, that would mean you're already in a risky position and would be at the mercy of the seller.

The contract details include:
- The purchase price.
- The completion date.
- Who is responsible for the various costs associated with the transaction, such as land registry fees, notary fees, taxes, estate agent fees, etc.
- Existing debts and liens to be resolved prior to the sale.
- Penalties for either party backing out of the contract.
- Conditions under which either party may withdraw.
- Details of the buyers and sellers.
- Property details.

You need to know that you have the mortgage for the property you want to buy before signing this. If your mortgage doesn't complete and you can't complete the property purchase, then you would lose your deposit. This risk will be minimised by following the advice of your lawyer and mortgage broker.

Once the bank issues a binding mortgage offer, there is a legally enforced ten-day cooling-off period. Ensure that you will have the funds available to cover your part of the purchase costs ready in time for completion, then you are ready to sign the PPC.

It has been suggested to us by professionals experienced with the Spanish mortgage process that **you could potentially apply for a loan in the U.K.** during the cooling-off period, **after** the binding mortgage offer is issued, if you have a shortfall in funds. Obviously, you would have to be certain that the loan will be available before the completion date else you are taking a huge risk of not completing the purchase and losing your deposit. However, this strategy is **highly risky** and probably violates the terms and conditions of your Spanish mortgage, so I do **not** recommend it.

9 - COMPLETION – NOTARY PUBLIC

So, the completion date has finally arrived! You are about to realise all your hard work to buy your dream property.

The completion meeting takes place at a notary's office. The final paperwork is signed, payment is made, and the property is legally transferred to you.

If you are present at the notary meeting, follow the notary's guidance. The notary or your lawyer will answer any questions you have. Your lawyer should select a bilingual notary. The notary is a public official who verifies the legality of the transaction and checks that you understand what you are signing. They will need a notarised copy of your passport and your NIE number.

In the U.K., lawyers handle the completion process between themselves, it's unusual for buyers and sellers to be present. They are just nervously expecting the solicitor's phone call to confirm completion, with the removal van waiting! In Spain, you can be present at the notary office if you wish to, or if you haven't granted your lawyer Power of Attorney (discussed in Chapter 6).

At least a week before completion, transfer the required funds to your Spanish bank providing the mortgage. Your lawyer will liaise with your Spanish bank, which will send you a breakdown of the amount to transfer. This is the sale price of the property less the mortgage, plus all expenses.

Your bank will then bring a cheque for the sale price, made out to the vendors, to the completion meeting. You will also need to pay the property transfer tax (or IVA for new properties).

The official property deed in Spain is called the *Escritura*. Both you and the vendor will sign this upon completion of the notary's legal checks. The notary will then register the deed with you as the new owner.

Once the formalities are complete, the keys to the property are handed over to you or your lawyer.

Your lawyer will notify utility companies of the ownership transfer and register your name(s). They can also set up direct debits if you desire, avoiding any potential service interruptions.

Remember to protect your new property:

- Change the door locks.
- Consider installing an alarm or CCTV (the latter may not be suitable for rental properties). Squatting can be an issue in Spain.
- Property insurance (buildings and contents), including civil liability. Arrange prior to completion to commence on the day of completion.
- Obtain a *nota simple* (property registry extract), this will take some time.
- Check the heating system and air conditioning.
- Smoke alarm.
- Internet connection.

Finally, book your flights and enjoy your new property!

10 - RENTING OUT THE PROPERTY - AN INTRODUCTION

The Affordability Calculator we used in chapter 3 has a final section called 'Rental income estimate' so you can estimate the potential reduction in your net outgoings if you were to rent out your property whilst vacant. This chapter introduces taking this step, with a focus on estimating your true cost of ownership. However, it isn't a guide on how to rent out your property which also requires various practical, legal and marketing steps.

Renting out your property while you can't use it will help reduce your total cost of ownership. When you're assessing properties to buy, you can also check rental values with agents. Estate agencies often also offer rental management services. Combined with your knowledge of rental rates paid whilst on holiday, you can make a good estimate.

Apartments / Pisos

Apartment rental management services offered by agents are another expensive item (you'll have spotted a theme here!). Fees are typically 25% of gross rent. However, negotiating with several agents can sometimes lower this cost. Also consider contacting property hosts who offered you good service during your own holiday rentals. Due to a rapidly changing regulatory landscape, there are restrictions on tourist rental apartments that do not apply to other property types.

Houses & Villas / Casas

Houses and villas will likely obtain licensing more easily compared to apartments, depending on the region. Costs will include advertising portal fees, hosting, property maintenance, and possibly higher insurance premiums due to the larger property size. Houses are more likely to be targeted towards short-term family holidays. This could make fitting-in your own use of the property quite flexible.

Tourist Rentals (up to 2 months)

Tourist licenses are mandatory in many regions of Spain for short-term tourist rentals of all property types. In recent years, there have been increasing restrictions on tourist licences for apartments in several regions. This has been widely reported in the news regarding Barcelona and Valencia. Catalunya has stringent regulations requiring community approval for tourist rentals. In Valencia there are similar restrictions aimed at managing high tourist traffic.

Due to recent regulatory changes in Málaga, no new tourist licenses are being issued for apartments. Here, and elsewhere, tourist licenses are issued to the owner and may not transfer with the property when sold.

Mid-Term Rentals (2 to 11 months)

Given the new regulations, an alternative is rentals of 2 to 11 months. These would often be for corporate clients or students.

There are several advantages of mid-term rentals, regardless of region. You'll have professional tenants who are likely to respect the property. Rental income is more stable. Agent fees may be lower than tourist rentals, starting as low as 8% (0.5 month's rental income for contracts up to 6 months), but these rates will vary.

However, be cautious of extending mid-term rentals into long-term ones over 1 year. Spanish law has strict tenant welfare regulations to protect tenancies over one year. Ensure thorough vetting of tenants, including checks on payslips and employment contracts.

Taxation

You should consult with a tax advisor to understand income tax, capital gains tax, and wealth tax implications. As a non-EU resident you will pay 24% income tax on the gross rental income, there are no allowable costs, unfortunately. At least you won't also be taxed on this income in the U.K. due to the Double Taxation Agreement between the U.K. and Spain.

Conclusion

Use the Affordability Calculator (see Chapter 3) to calculate your ongoing monthly net costs. These are the mortgage payments less rental income after income tax, rental agent fees and maintenance costs. This rental income will reduce the net monthly cost of your affordable dream home in Spain!

Once the mortgage is paid-off you will hopefully have found that your property has also been a good investment and delivered on your dreams for many years. Congratulations for making it this far and thank you for reading! ¡Felicidades!

Printed in Great Britain
by Amazon